KT-573-912

DAVID BOWIE
STARMAN

DAVID BOWIE
STARMAN

Illustrations by Coco Balderrama

Text by Laura Coulman

Plexus, London

DAVID BOWIE'S STYLE LEGACY

"HE STOLE IDEAS FROM EVERYWHERE"

By Sheryl Garratt

In 2012, I visited the V&A's costume preservation department to see the preparations for the museum's record-breaking David Bowie retrospective the following year. A curator carefully unwrapped the tissue paper around one garment and laid it out for me to see. It was an item as familiar to me as the school uniform I wore for my first five years of secondary school and, indeed, a picture of Bowie wearing it has been on my bedroom wall for most of that time: a knitted jumpsuit in a bright zigzag pattern, with one leg cut off at the upper thigh and one arm cut away to reveal bare shoulder. It was, of course, a stage outfit he wore during his Ziggy Stardust/Aladdin Sane tours, and the biggest surprise about it for me, close-up, was that it was knitted, with quite thick wool in the most richly patterned parts.

I remarked that it must have been ridiculously hot to wear during a frenetic live show, and the curators laughed and said that sweat damage was one of the main problems they were working on with the stage clothes. (The original jumpsuit, for instance, had long since rotted away and the one shown at the V&A had actually been recreated by its designer, Kansai Yamamoto, for an exhibition in New York a few years earlier.)

Later, I got to talk to Yamamoto on the phone and he told me about the first time he saw Bowie wear his clothes on stage, in a 1973 show at the Radio City Music Hall in New York. 'There's a time difference of thirteen hours between Tokyo and New York, but a good friend of mine phoned me in Japan many times through the night, saying, "There's this very interesting person called David Bowie here in New York. You've got to see him. Fly over immediately!" If somebody calls you again and again at 3am, it must really be pretty interesting. So I cancelled all other plans for that week, and got on a plane to see his show.

'I'd never seen a performance like it. When the show started, he came down from the ceiling, wearing clothes I had designed. Then there was a movement that often occurs in *kabuki*, which is called *hikinuki*, where somebody is wearing one costume and it is stripped off, immediately revealing what is underneath. So he was wearing all black and then all of a sudden that disappeared, and he was wearing full colour. It was very dramatic, and the audience all rose to their feet, so there was a standing ovation right at the beginning.

'My clothes were normally made for professional models – this was the first time they had been used for an artist or singer. It felt like the beginning of a new age.'

The two men became friends, and later that year met up in Tokyo to collaborate on more stage outfits, including the knitted jumpsuit. Yamamoto helped Bowie gain a deeper understanding of the Japanese culture that so fascinated him, taking him to dinner with the revered *kabuki* actor Bando Tamasaburo, for instance. Through Bowie, Yamamoto says he learned to present his designs more theatrically and start a second career as a producer. 'Throughout this time, we were always bouncing off each other, inspiring each other.'

The jumpsuit, meanwhile, has echoed through fashion ever since, from the '80s designs of Bodymap to the knitted leggings every teenage girl was sporting last winter.

There are stories like this from almost every year of Bowie's long career. He was the first, the original and the best pop chameleon, ringing the ch-ch-changes for every new release or tour, playing with costume, masks and alter egos in a way that always felt organic and interesting. He stole ideas from everywhere and was a great collaborator, pushing almost everyone he worked with to do their best work, but Bowie was always unmistakably Bowie, adding his own distinctive sense of style into the mix.

He and his glam-rock contemporary Marc Bolan probably did more than anyone to introduce androgyny into the mainstream, as well as the idea that sexuality could be far more fluid and flexible than we had been taught.

'I was living in Paris when I first experienced Bowie's music, and the influence was instant and permanent,' Jean Paul Gaultier wrote on *Out* magazine's website. 'He was in a dress for the sleeve of *The Man Who Sold the World* – there was a sense of ambiguity and originality that was incredible at the time . . . I remember

'He stole ideas from everywhere and was a great collaborator, pushing almost everyone he worked with to do their best work, but Bowie was always unmistakably Bowie, adding his own distinctive sense of style into the mix. '

going to gay bars in London that Bowie was known to frequent and it gave many of us courage not to hide, to have confidence in ourselves.'

In 1975 Bowie veered off into new territory, exploring his love of Philly soul with the *Young Americans* album, and introducing a look that has echoed through both gay clubs and soul weekenders ever since: the extravagant quiff or dyed wedge cut, teamed with a tailored shirt and baggy trousers. A year later, with *Station to Station*, he created his last great character, the Thin White Duke, whose louche, suited look has influenced menswear ever since.

In 1980 he adopted a New Romantic Pierrot guise for *Scary Monsters (and Super Creeps)*, an album explicitly reclaiming ground that had been occupied by club kids who had grown up

> **'**For us, a new Bowie album was not just a collection of songs; it was a doorway to new images, books, art, cultural references and sounds. We pored over his interviews and influences, and made them our own. **,**

under his influence. After that he lost his way a little, but it barely mattered: he had changed popular culture indelibly.

There was no internet when I was in my teens. For us, a new Bowie album was not just a collection of songs; it was a doorway to new images, books, art, cultural references and sounds. We pored over his interviews and influences, and made them our own. Although I never did get the chiselled cheekbones I so longed for, through Bowie I learned about Lindsay Kemp and Aleister Crowley, about Iggy Pop and Nietzsche, about Kraftwerk and *kabuki*, and all kinds of other things besides.

I'm not alone in this, of course. Which is why Bowie has been so influential across our culture, and nowhere more so than fashion. Bowie's 1980 track 'Fashion' has provided the soundtrack for more catwalk shows than

I could ever hope to list here and, of course, Bowie made a cameo appearance – judging a walk-off between two competing male models – in Ben Stiller's brilliant 2001 fashion spoof *Zoolander*. In 2014, he even appeared in a fashion ad himself, crooning seductively to the model Arizona Muse for Louis Vuitton. ('He was so lovely,' Muse told me afterwards. 'Very charming and easy to talk to, with a really nice, calm energy.')

Lady Gaga makes explicit reference to Bowie in both her 'Applause' and 'Just Dance' videos, while Kate Moss – that most reliable barometer of all that is best in British style – has dressed as Bowie twice: for British *Vogue* in 2003, and for French *Vogue* in 2011. In 2014, she did it again, picking up a BRIT award on Bowie's behalf dressed in one of Yamamoto's actual Ziggy Stardust costumes.

But this is mere surface and Bowie's

influence is deep in the DNA of contemporary fashion. To celebrate his 69th birthday – sadly only two days before his death – several fashion websites pointed to his influence on recent catwalk shows, for both men's and women's collections. Givenchy's spring 2010 ready-to-wear show, for instance, featured a striped blazer that is a clear homage to a Freddie Burretti one sported by Bowie in 1973; a year later, Lanvin's autumn 2011 show saw models dressed in wide-brimmed fedoras like Bowie in *The Man Who Fell to Earth*. Balmain's collection had an Aladdin Sane jumpsuit, while Walter Van Beirendonck had a blazer adorned with a clever Aladdin Sane diagonal flash across the lapels, and Dries Van Noten and Alber Elbaz's autumn menswear shows both heavily referenced the Thin White Duke.

In 2012 Emilio Pucci had jewel-bright suits with more than a hint of Bowie about them, while Alexander McQueen had wide trousers straight from Bowie's *Hunky Dory* period.

Jean Paul Gaultier, who used 'Diamond Dogs' to open his first show for Pierre Cardin in 1975, has returned to this fertile creative ground again and again, paying homage to Kansai Yamamoto's colourful prints in spring 2011, and revisiting the one-legged jumpsuit in 2013, both times lovingly acknowledging the reference by sending out his models in flaming red mullets.

Hedi Slimane – another huge fan who claimed, in 2010, 'I was literally born with a David Bowie album in my hand' – last referenced the Thin White Duke in his spring '14 collection for Saint Laurent. A year later, Raf Simons made a nod to Yamamoto's jumpsuits in his spring 2015 couture collection for Dior, while Jun Takahashi recreated the cover of *Heroes* for his 'Undercover Fall '15' menswear lookbook.

Most of all, what Bowie did was give generations of teens who didn't feel like they

> ❛ What Bowie did was give generations of teens who didn't feel like they fitted in permission to be different and some ideas to start playing with while they found identities of their own. ❜

fitted in permission to be different and some ideas to start playing with while they found identities of their own. Creativity always finds an expression and it would be absurd to suggest that without him, we wouldn't have Boy George or Lady Gaga, Gaultier or Slimane. But had Bowie not existed, it would all look, sound and feel slightly different.

Speaking at the launch party for the V&A exhibition, Tilda Swinton admitted it was the image, not the music, that first drew her into Bowie's world. 'When I was twelve . . . I carried a copy of *Aladdin Sane* around with me – a full two years before I had the wherewithal to play it,' she said.

'The image of that gingery, bony, pinky-whitey person on the cover with the liquid mercury collar bone was – for one particular young moonage daydreamer – the image of planetary kin, of a close imaginary cousin and companion of choice.

'I'm not saying that if you hadn't pitched up I would have worn a pie-crust collar and pearls like some of those I went to school with. I'm not saying that if you hadn't weighed in, [the London DJ and club icon] Princess Julia would have been less inventive with the pink blusher. Simply that you provided the sideways like us with such rare and out-there company, such fellowship; you pulled us in and left your arm dangling over our necks, and kept us warm.'

REMEMBERING DAVID BOWIE

❝David's friendship was the light of my life.
I never met such a brilliant person.
He was the best there is.❞ – Iggy Pop

❝An amazing life. An amazing career.❞ – Elton John

❝David was always
an inspiration to me
and a true original.
He was wonderfully
shameless in his work.
He was my friend.
I will never forget him.❞
– Mick Jagger

❝What a lucky planet we
were to have had David
Bowie . . . a joyful alien,
singing songs directly to –
and for – anyone who
felt weird, or lonely . . .
a man so effortlessly able
to write the songs of
the human heart.❞
– Caitlin Moran

❝His star will shine in the sky forever.❞ – Paul McCartney

'Who doesn't love Bowie? A visionary artist, musician, actor, a completely renaissance man . . . I can't say enough about David Bowie to show how much I love him.' – Debbie Harry

'David Bowie was one of my most important inspirations, so fearless, so creative. He gave us magic for a lifetime.' – Kanye West

'Please could every radio station around the globe just play David Bowie music today – I think the world owes him that.' – Eddie Izzard

'He was a fearsome talent, and the loss to music and culture from his passing is inestimable. All hail, David Bowie, Star Man, Hero. RIP.' – Brian May

'I just lost a hero. RIP David Bowie.' – Ricky Gervais

'Right now, it feels as if the solar system is off its axis. That said – I am certain that wherever Bowie is now – I want to be there someday.' – Michael Stipe, R.E.M.

'He always did what he wanted to do. And he wanted to do it his way and he wanted to do it the best way. His death was no different from his life – a work of art. He made *Blackstar* for us, his parting gift . . . He was an extraordinary man, full of love and life. He will always be with us. For now, it is appropriate to cry.' – Tony Visconti, producer for Bowie

'When a true star blinks out, the sky looks different and never feels the same.' – Billy Corgan, Smashing Pumpkins

'It's almost impossible to mention Bowie's name in the past tense. Everything he represented as an artist will always be vital and incredibly present.' – Annie Lennox

'Over his career, David challenged and changed our understanding of the medium, whether in music or in life, he emphasised originality, experimentation, exploration and in his very unique way, he also reminded us to never take ourselves too seriously.' – Gary Oldman

❛ Everything I've read or seen since the news has been deeply intrinsic in tone, almost selfish, like therapy. That's who he was to all of us. He was a piece of bright pleated silk we could stretch out or fold up small inside ourselves when we needed to. Mr Bowie, I guess right now we have to hang this thing up for a minute. ❜ – Lorde

❛ Let's celebrate his life more than mourn his passing . . . All things must pass and all that . . . He was quite fearless, which is one of the things that I will remember him for – taking his art, always moving it forward. ❜
– Noel Gallagher

❛ I didn't think we were done. It feels like the loss of a mentor, fatherly figure, someone looking out for you, reminding you that in a world where the bar keeps seeming to be lower, where stupidity has got a foothold, there is room for excellence and uncompromising vision. ❜
– Trent Reznor, Nine Inch Nails

❛ Immortal unbelievable. A gentleman and a hero. ❜
– Massive Attack

❛ Talented. Unique. Genius. Game changer. The man who fell to Earth. Your spirit lives on forever! ❜
– Madonna

‘Bowie existed so all of us misfits learned that an oddity was a precious thing; he changed the world forever.’ – Guillermo del Toro

‘My whole young life I laid on the carpet in my room listening to Bowie . . . feeling my mind and heart open up inspired me more than I can express.’
– Edward Norton

‘Thank God David Bowie walked the earth and thank God we were able to experience what he had to give.’
– Kirk Hammett, Metallica

‘He is a true, true artist and I . . . just know that you can use the theatre of your imagination to entertain people beyond their wildest dreams and then you can put something inside of that that changes the world, and that to me is when you make something truly great as an artist.’ – Lady Gaga

‘We were so thrilled to have him back we failed to notice he was saying goodbye.’ – Graeme Thomson, writer

'I received an email from him seven days ago. It was as funny as always, and as surreal, looping through word games and allusions and all the usual stuff we did. It ended with this sentence: "Thank you for our good times, Brian. They will never rot." And it was signed "Dawn". I realise now he was saying goodbye.' – Brian Eno

'In life, there's only one rule: don't trust anyone who doesn't like David Bowie.'
– Miranda Sawyer, journalist

'I feel so lucky to have considered you a friend.RIP. Thank you for everything.'
– Sean Lennon

'For those who were his fans he was a charismatic and exotic creature and still gloriously beautiful even as he approached 70. But face to face he was funny, clever, well-read, excited by the arts, and really good company . . . We have lost a monumental figurehead of the British arts scene. We have also lost a wonderful clown whose combined sense of mischief and creativity delightedly touched our hearts. David Bowie was my Salvador Dali. He was also one facet of my perfect Ace Face.' – Pete Townshend

CAN'T HELP THINKING ABOUT ME

‘ My real name is Davie Jones . . .
and I don't have to tell you why I changed it. ’
– David Bowie, early letter to a young fan

From the King Bee to Manish Boy, from Konrad to Lower Third, from sharp-suited young Mod to whimsical (and somewhat persecuted) blond-locked folkster, Davie Jones spent much of the sixties experimenting with different genres and styles, drifting in and out of various South London bands with a view to seizing creative control for himself . . . till the world could no longer ignore his music. Though virtually penniless, Davie was lacking in neither talent nor dedication (when he wasn't frantically writing new material in the hope of generating his

‘ I've been the male equivalent of a dumb blond for a few years, and I was beginning to despair of people accepting me. ’
– David Bowie

‘ I often regret not leading a more normal teenage life. From the time I was about sixteen, I never kicked a football over a common with my mates, I haven't had to chat up a girl like an ordinary teenager for ages and believe it or not I miss it. ’
– David Bowie

breakthrough hit, he was to be found touring venues across the country in his clapped-out ambulance-cum-mobile home). Yet without his slick new moniker – borrowed from the wickedly glinting Bowie knife – and electrifying avant-garde performance personas, he was fated to go unnoticed, amidst a legion of other struggling wannabes on the London scene.

PIERROT IN TURQUOISE

The year was 1966 and David was in a fug of disillusionment, almost ready to give up on the music business altogether. Then he met travelling mime Lindsay Kemp and everything changed. 'It was love at first sight . . . he fell for the bohemianism of my world,' revealed Kemp with a glint. Besotted by the heady combination of music, dance and performance, David threw himself wholeheartedly into lessons at Kemp's Covent

‘ I taught David to free his body. Even before meeting, David and I had felt the need to work together. I'd identified myself with his songs, and he'd seen my performances and identified himself with my songs. I was singing the songs of my life with my body; he was singing the songs of his life very fabulously with his voice, and we reckoned that by putting the two together the audience couldn't help but be enthralled. In other words, one large gin is very nice, but two large gins are even nicer. ’

– Lindsay Kemp

‘ We know what can happen: you can get a job, go to work . . . follow that line of perceived security. But I think there's a different kind of security . . . of almost drifting where the wind takes you. And I spent well into my twenties doing that – throwing myself wholeheartedly into life at every avenue and seeing what happened. ’

– David Bowie

Garden-based dance school. 'David was a huge hit with the ladies,' adds Kemp, 'improvising sailors drowning at sea, animals hunting their prey. Those ladies would have devoured him like the Maenads.' And it wasn't only the ladies who were smitten. Before long, Kemp had persuaded his 'A student' – with whom he discussed *kabuki*, music hall and all things avant-garde – into staging a whimsical musical fancy named *Pierrot in Turquoise*. The show opened at Oxford Playhouse in December 1967, with David's original songs for the dreamlike soundtrack and a TV version, *The Looking Glass Murders* to follow. Appearing as 'Cloud' – a pale-faced balladeer whose eloquent features were expressive beyond words – David was a haunting revelation.

CELESTIAL BODIES IN MOTION

GROUND CONTROL TO MAJOR TOM . . .

' In England, it was always presumed that the song was written about the space landing . . . but it actually wasn't. It was written because of the film *2001: A Space Odyssey* [Stanley Kubrick, 1968], which I found amazing. I was out of my gourd . . . very stoned when I went to see it and it was really a revelation to me. It got the song flowing. It was picked up by British television and used as background music for the landing itself. I'm sure they really weren't listening to the lyric at all. '

– David Bowie

With his visor-like shades and nebulous cloud of curls, David is impossible to separate from the protein-addled protagonist of 'Space Oddity'. Telling of beleaguered astronaut Major Tom, this 1969 ballad – awash with sweetly spaced-out harmonies – was the song to finally launch Bowie's career to the stars . . . as well as an actual rocket! To the excitement of all concerned, Bowie's label rushed to release the single on 11 July 1969 – days before the launch of Apollo 11. When the BBC selected the paranoid anthem as part of their coverage of the mission to the moon, the irony was not lost on David himself.

' Some of it belonged in '67 and some of it in '72, but in 1969 it all seemed vastly incongruous. Basically, *David Bowie* can be viewed in retrospect as all that Bowie had been and a little of what he would become, all jumbled up and fighting for control. '

– Roy Carr and Charles Shaar Murray, *NME*

A DARKNESS IN THE DNA?

'He was very pretty.
Beautiful, actually: his
hair cut and permed in
tight little curls around
that fallen-angel's face.'
– Angie Bowie,
Backstage Passes

WITH THE MAN WHO SOLD THE WORLD

‘ I guess I wrote 'The Man Who Sold the World' because there was a part of myself that I was looking for . . . That song for me always exemplified how you feel when you're young, when you know that there's a piece of yourself that you haven't really put together yet. You have this great searching; this need to find out who you really are. ,

– David Bowie

It wasn't until April 1971 – and the release of the UK edition of *The Man Who Sold the World* – that David truly began exploring his gift for visual display to the full. Sprawled nonchalantly across a couch, amidst the opulent confines of Haddon Hall (a grandly decaying Edwardian mansion in Beckenham), his hair falling in soft waves and his slender frame clad in a gorgeous velveteen gown by London designer Michael Fish, Bowie cuts a most bewitching, bewildering figure. Hazy as a Pre-Raphaelite dream, his appearance on the UK album cover (replaced in the US by a reassuringly muscular cartoon cowboy) belies the heavy guitar sound and the lyrical content (there's not a hint of truth in the haunting title track, only a darkening blur of conflicting assertions). In the scope of David's career, this daring, androgynous style statement marks a turning point. 'I refuse to be thought of as mediocre,' Bowie stated in *Rolling Stone*, the same month that his dress-clad artwork shot shocked the world. 'If I am mediocre, I'll get out of the business. There's enough fog around. That's why the idea of performance-as-spectacle is so important to me.' He made these his words to live by ever after.

HE SELLS SANCTUARY

PRETTY KOOKY TOO

' I thrive on mistakes.
If I haven't made three good mistakes
in a week, then I'm not worth anything.
You only learn from mistakes. '
– David Bowie

The year was 1971. And David had already proven himself to be a shape-shifting fashion chameleon. Strung-out space cadet; lunar-looking mime; damsel in a dress – he'd appeared in all these guises and more besides. Yet, even by Bowie's standards of self-styled kook, Brian Ward's original vision for the cover of *Hunky Dory* seemed a step too far. Like the rest of London's populace – feverishly anticipating the arrival of the treasures of Tutankhamun at the British Museum – Ward was in thrall to the ferocious majesty of the Pharaohs. Somehow, he persuaded Bowie to partake in an Egyptian-themed photo-shoot, clad in a lime green headdress and dripping with gold accessories. A wide-eyed, Nile-side nightmare, the result was undeniably hypnotic, but utterly unsuitable for the album sleeve. Despite Bowie's 'plans to appear on-stage decked out like Cleopatra' (also eventually shelved), the pair settled on a cover that was more of the moment, rather than buried millennia in the sands of the past.

' I find that I am a
person who can
take on the guises
of different people that
I meet . . . I always
found that I collect;
I am a collector, and
I've always just
seemed to collect
personalities. '
– David Bowie

CURSE OF THE PHARAOHS

OH, YOU PRETTY THING . . .

' I fell for Ziggy too. It was quite easy to become obsessed night and day with the character. I became Ziggy Stardust. David Bowie went totally out the window. Everybody was convincing me that I was a Messiah . . . I got hopelessly lost in the fantasy. '
– David Bowie

The very last word in circuit-board chic, Bowie's flamboyant cap and suit (designed by irresistible *beau de nuit* Freddie Burretti) are hardly appropriate attire for painting houses. Yet this is exactly what Bowie was wearing – and occupied with – whilst entertaining photographer Michael Putland at Haddon Hall in 1972. At this time, Bowie was slipping deep under the skin of his first ever stage persona: the doomed alien rock god, Ziggy Stardust. A hedonistic

' Until that time, the attitude was, "What you see is what you get." It seemed interesting to try to devise something different, like a musical where the artist on-stage plays a part. '
– David Bowie

messenger sent to warn earthlings of the coming apocalypse, Ziggy's snow-white skin, infectious riffs and other 'god-given' attributes worked like a charm upon the hysterical, hormonal masses. By summer of that same year, the planet belonged to Ziggy. Of all Earth's inhabitants, few could claim immunity to the otherworldly siren song of Ziggy and his Spiders from Mars – and Bowie himself was certainly not one of them.

' Freddie, my designer, is extremely patient. He just listens to my ideas and has this sort of telepathy, because whatever I think of in my mind he produces for real. I just hope he'll continue to design incredible clothes for me. '
– David Bowie

HE THINKS HE'D BLOW OUR MINDS

❛ I always had a repulsive need to be something more than human. I felt very, very puny as a human. I thought, "F*** that. I want to be superhuman." ❜

– David Bowie

One day in January 1972, *Melody Maker* writer Michael Watts reports to a tiny office, high above the rush of Regent Street. There, he awaits David Bowie, fey and fascinating folk rocker. Except it isn't *Bowie* who comes to greet him. 'Dolled up' in an eye-popping, 'skin-tight pantsuit' and sky-high cherry platform boots, Ziggy Stardust was the only ego in attendance that day. Further headline-grabbing revelations followed. 'I'm

❛ As an adolescent, I was painfully shy; withdrawn. I didn't really have the nerve to sing my songs on-stage . . . I decided to do them in disguise so that I didn't have to actually go through the humiliation of going on-stage and being myself. I continued designing characters with their own complete personalities. Rather than be me – which must be incredibly boring to anyone – I'd take Ziggy into interviews with me. ❜

– David Bowie

❛ Now, of course, Yamamoto is an international designer, but he was very experimental then – way off the board . . . and he made all the stuff you really know: the suits, the pull-apart stuff. He said, "Oh, this band are weird – *tee-hee-hee* – and they wear my clothes." ❜

– David Bowie

gay. Always have been,' Ziggy came out moments into the interview. A mere five years after the reform of bigoted UK law, it was a daring admission. Yet David was as much in control of his ambiguous alien sexuality as every other aspect of his outrageous new persona – including Ziggy's arsenal of stacked and spangled spacesuits. The glitter-encrusted fancy pictured here comes courtesy of Kansai Yamamoto, whose exotic Eastern-tinged designs couldn't help but catch David's magpie eye. In shaping Ziggy's nebulous stardusted form into the vivid vision he became, Yamamoto's influence was second to none.

WATCH THIS CREATURE FAIR . . .

Ziggy may be synonymous with glacially cool tailoring, but this achingly cute little playsuit is as iconic as any of the suits in Ziggy's performance wardrobe. Perfect for strutting and shimmying his way seductively across the stage, its terracotta fabric is adorned with swirls and wide-eyed woodland creatures so adorable that they wouldn't look out of place frolicking alongside Disney's Bambi. Custom-made by Kansai Yamamoto and debuted by Bowie on 19 August 1972 on-stage at the Rainbow, the suit is the very embodiment of androgynous

❛In Japanese myth, the rabbits on my old costume that Kate's wearing actually live on the moon. Kate comes from Venus and I'm from Mars, so that's nice! I'm completely delighted to have a BRIT for being the best male. But I am, aren't I, Kate? Thank you very, very much.❜
– David Bowie

❛I never do anything by halves. The costumes for the act are outrageous. I've had twelve, fifteen made up . . . I'm out to bloody well entertain, not just get up on-stage and knock out a few songs. I couldn't live with myself if I did that. I'm the last person to pretend I'm a radio. I'd rather go out and be a colour television set.❜
– David Bowie

Lolita-tinged chic. Needless to say, it was rocked by Bowie on many further occasions before Ziggy took his final bow (or curtsy) at the Hammersmith Odeon in 1973. Four decades on, the creatures were given a long overdue outing at the 2014 BRIT Awards, where they were seen draped across another similarly delicate frame: that of ubiquitous couture queen, Kate Moss.

THE STARMAN SPEAKS

KEEP YOUR ELECTRIC EYE ON ME, BABE!

' I actually had no idea who David Bowie was until I saw him wearing my clothes onstage in New York . . . the first time I ever met an artist wearing my designs. I didn't know how immensely talented he was. At the time he was all about transcending gender . . . I remember thinking *whoa* when I saw him wearing clothes I had designed for women. The clothes were influenced by *hikinuki*, the method of changing costumes quickly in *kabuki* [Japanese dance-drama]. The audience saw the costumes transform . . . I realised I had done something really cool when everyone got on their feet and clapped. '

– Kansai Yamamoto

Beamed straight from the futuristic imagination of Kansai Yamamoto, this iridescent, asymmetric jumpsuit became one of Bowie's most thrilling staple looks on the Ziggy Stardust/Aladdin Sane tour (running from 1972 to '73). Draped in a decadent silken kimono (some of which came with a staggering £600-price tag), Ziggy would come sashaying effortlessly on to the stage . . . only to cast off the voluminous garment several numbers in, to breathtaking effect. Beneath, he'd be clad in nothing but a similarly skimpy one-piece. Emblazoned with intensely intricate rainbow patterning – reminiscent of the tribal tattoos of the Japanese *yakuza* – Bowie's second-skin was knitted from neon wool of the most luxuriant consistency – less than ideal for Ziggy's attention-grabbing antics beneath the hot stage lighting, but what did the supremely superficial Martian care about that? Sweat-damaged beyond repair, the seventies originals have long since rotted away, though Yamamoto has been known to knit one-off modern-day replicas . . .

'Sometimes I don't feel as if I'm a person at all. I'm just a collection of other people's ideas.'
– David Bowie

ALL THE YOUNG DUDES

By 3 July 1973, Bowie had been on the road for a solid year. Comet-like, Ziggy had blazed a trail from London to Liverpool, NYC to New Orleans, Texas to Tokyo – and back to London's Hammersmith Odeon. Somewhere between, the shimmer had worn off for Bowie himself. 'There was a point in '73 where I knew it was all over,' he sighed. 'I didn't want to be trapped in this character all my life.' Henceforth, the fate of Ziggy and his Spiders was sealed. 'This show

❛Aladdin was meant to be a crossover: getting out of Ziggy and not really knowing where I was going. It was a little ephemeral 'cause it was certainly up in the air. I guess what I was doing was . . . using a rather pale imitation of Ziggy as a secondary device. In my mind it was Ziggy goes to Washington; Ziggy under the influence of America.❜
– David Bowie

❛Instead of the flame of a lamp, I thought he would probably be cracked by lightning . . . as he was sort of an electric boy. The teardrop was Brian Duffy's [photographer] . . . I thought it was rather sweet.❜
– David Bowie

will stay longest in our memories,' Bowie told the Hammersmith crowd before the final encore of 'Rock'n'Roll Suicide'. 'Not just because it is the end of the tour, but because it is the last show we'll ever do.' And so, Ziggy's star imploded most spectacularly . . . before long, the void he left was filled with a dazzling new persona. With stardust in his eyes and rosy, lightning-struck features, Aladdin Sane was not unlike the alien rock god Bowie had just retired – but marked with a dark-and-dangerous streak as vivid as the neon bolt slashed across his deathly white forehead.

A LAD INSANE?

JEAN GENIE,
LET YOURSELF GO!

'I found a lightning bolt really represented Aladdin.'
– David Bowie

Whatever their superficial similarities make no mistake: Ziggy and Aladdin are two very different beasts, dancing to equally different beats. A washed-up Hollywood has-been who haunts the seediest corners of Sunset and Vine, Aladdin was in dire need of a wardrobe of his own – reflective of the uniquely depraved scene that spawned him. Thankfully, Kansai Yamamoto was more than equal to the challenge of dressing Bowie's curiously cracked actor for the stage. This 'Tokyo Pop' bodysuit – cut from slick black vinyl with

'When David visited Tokyo, I took him to a market and he was delighted with an over-the-shoulder bag . . . actually it was made for Japanese bus drivers! How would I describe him? Sensitive, bold and dynamic.'
– Kansai Yamamoto

'Aladdin Sane was a schizophrenic – that accounted for lots of it, why there were so many costume changes, because he had so many personalities. As far as I was concerned, each costume change was a different facet of a personality.'
– David Bowie

spectacular space-age sheen – was custom-made by Yamamoto in 1973 and became one of Aladdin's most iconic ever looks. Ballooning out to form one giant stripy bell-bottom, the suit's loose fit made it a perfect choice for Bowie's *kabuki*-inspired live shows.

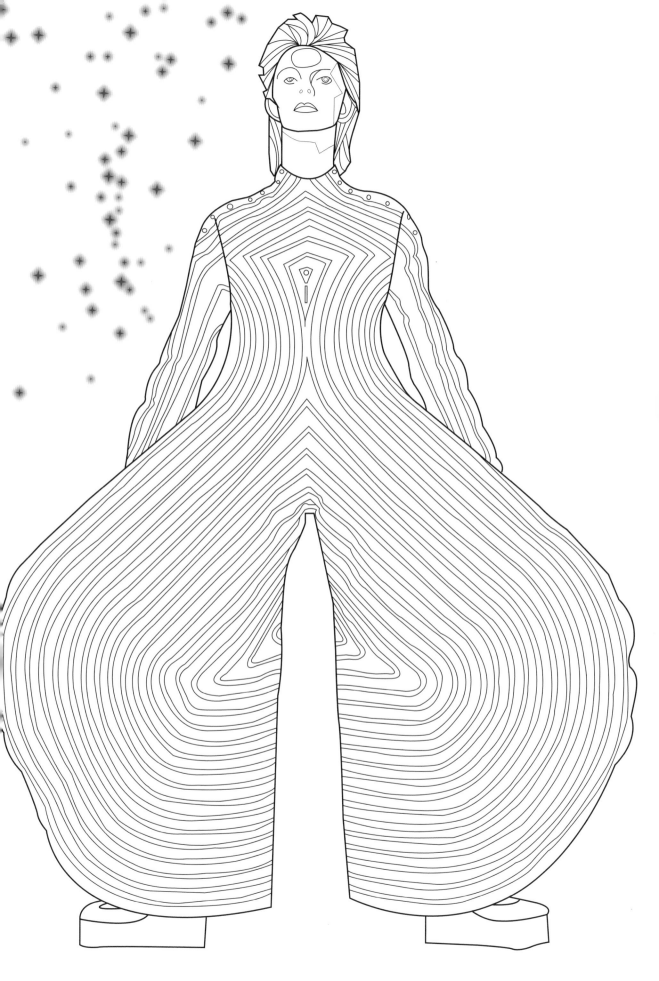

YOU'LL LOSE YOUR MIND AND PLAY

Bowie's shock announcement at the Hammersmith Odeon – the 'last show we'll ever do' – came as less of a bombshell and more of a celestial event. Rather than endure the fall-out, Bowie opted to escape to the French countryside. In this sundrenched refuge, he planned to record an album of covers, lovingly selected from 'all the bands which I used to go and hear play down the Marquee between 1964 and 1967'. From the mournful melodies of the McCoys' 'Sorrow' – to which Bowie added soaring strings and excess attitude – to the crazed jangling maelstrom of 'See Emily Play' (an hallucinogenic Syd Barrett original), the sixties classics selected for the album were 'all very dear' to Bowie – a sonic map to show his own personal London 'of the time'.

Situated just north of Paris, Bowie's chosen venue for recording was the George Sand studio, within the fairytale confines of the Château d'Hérouville. Said to be haunted by the amorous ghosts of Frédéric Chopin and his mistress, this swinging country pile became a Mecca for everyone from Fleetwood Mac to the Bee Gees. The iconic cover features a barely recognisable Twiggy – the model muse's hair swept back and her eyes painted in starry metallic shades to match David's own brand of futuristic alien chic.

'There was certainly some strange energy in that château. On the first day David took one look at the master bedroom and said, "I'm not sleeping in there!" It felt like it was haunted as all f***, but what could Chopin and Sand really do to me? Scare me in French? I loved the look of the room so I decided to spend one night there. If something happened I planned to shout so loud I'd wake up the village. '

– Tony Visconti

STRIKE A POSE

❛ [Twiggy and I] met Bowie and he mentioned that he wanted to be the first man on the cover of *Vogue*. I called them to suggest this . . . and after a bit of a hoo-ha, they agreed. To be honest, I wasn't a professional photographer . . . Bowie was working on *Pin Ups* in Paris, so we flew there to do the shoot. When Twigs and Bowie were together and lit up, I looked through the viewfinder and realised that David was pure white, whereas Twiggy was tanned from a holiday in Bermuda. There was a moment of panic because I knew it would look bizarre; but the makeup artist suggested drawing masks on them, and this worked out even better.

'I remember distinctly that I'd got it with the first shot. It was too good to be true. When I showed Bowie the test Polaroids, he asked if he could use it for the *Pin Ups* record sleeve . . . When I got back to London and told *Vogue*, they never spoke to me again. Several weeks later, Twigs and I were driving along Sunset Boulevard and we passed a 60ft billboard of the picture. I knew I had made the right decision. ❜

– Justin de Villeneuve, Twiggy's boyfriend/manager

BETTER HANG ON TO YOURSELF

'Ziggy was dead, but not quite buried . . .'
– Dave Thompson, *Moonage Daydream*

Even in November 1973, with the Spiders in retirement and Bowie masquerading as a high fashion *Pin Up*, the spectre of Ziggy still hangs about his flame-haired creator. In the cut of his jacket and the bizarrely beautiful feather collar at his throat – giving Bowie the look of a surreal, space-faring Aztec – Ziggy's influence can be felt.

Yet beneath the plumage of his former personas (Ziggy and Aladdin), David was refining the concept for a thrilling new artistic venture . . . distilled from an array of new inspirations. From his recent Russian odyssey by rail ('there's very little to talk about, apart from the people,' David shrugged) and his love for George Orwell's darkened dystopian vision, *1984*, the germ of an idea was taking shape. Soon, Bowie would come to realise that 1974 was to be the year of the Diamond Dogs.

'It's okay as long as you're really in control of the image, as a painter is, for instance. But when you're using yourself as the image it's never quite as simple as that . . . aspects of your own life get mixed into the image that you're trying to project as a character, so it becomes a hybrid of reality and fantasy. And that is an extraordinary situation. Then the awareness that that's not the real you and you're uncomfortable having to pretend that it is makes you withdraw. And I withdrew . . .'
– David Bowie

BLURRED BEINGS

REBEL REBEL, HOW COULD THEY KNOW?

With Ziggy's star officially burned to dust, it was only a matter of time before David found himself in the grip (or perhaps the jaws?) of an all-consuming new obsession. Enter Halloween Jack, trash-talking anti-hero of Bowie's 1974 concept album, *Diamond Dogs*. Straight from the depraved streets of Hunger City (whose infernal, dystopian skyline bears more than a passing resemblance to that of NYC), Jack gets his kicks wherever – and with whomever – he can. Yet even Jack can't cheat death forever . . .

Part-dog, part-human and entirely male (as revealed in a flash of canine anatomy), his hybrid form was captured in garish neon colour by Belgian artist Guy Peellaert – for Bowie's most scandalous album cover yet. Having tempted Peellaert away from a commission with Mick Jagger, Bowie revelled in the controversy caused by his latest lurid, lounging mutation. Though the dog's genitalia had to be tastefully airbrushed out for later printings of the album, Bowie's darkened apocalyptic vision remained, razor-sharp incisors intact.

'John Lennon was around at that time, and every now and then the camera catches sight of him in the background, sitting there with his guitar playing hits of the day and saying, "what the bloody hell are you doing, Bowie? It's all so negative, your shit. All this *Diamond Dogs* mutant crap. Ha, ha, ha."

– David Bowie

DIAMOND DISSENTER?

'*Diamond Dogs* is a very political album.

My protest . . . more than anything

I've done previously. '

– David Bowie

ZIGGY PLAYED GUITAR

' Imagine a tracking shot across the universe . . . as it scrolls past, you can hear "Rebel Rebel" coming from our planet, from our country, playing on tinny transistor radios in a million bedrooms, as a whole generation, and the next, and the next, straighten their spines, and feel their pulses rise, and say: "This. This is how I feel. Or at least, this is how I feel now. Now I've heard this." '

– Caitlin Moran

A swaggering glam-rock anthem – dedicated to one spectacularly hot mess of a protagonist – 'Rebel Rebel' was (and always will be) beloved by fabulously dishevelled misfits everywhere. Yet, that the track came into being at all is nothing but a glorious cosmic accident. Bowie himself revealed: 'One night, I was in a London hotel trying to get some sleep . . . I heard this riff being played really badly from upstairs. I thought, "Who the hell is doing this at this time of night?" On an electric guitar, over and over. So, I went upstairs to show the person how to play the thing. I bang on the door. It opens and I say, "Listen, if you're going to play . . ." and it was John McEnroe [tennis champion]! I kid you not. That could only happen in a movie, couldn't it?'

For a once-in-a-lifetime rendition of the song on Dutch TV (pictured here), David opted to appear in the guise of a red-hot rebel pirate – complete with natty neckerchief and breeches so bright they matched his flaming red mullet. His eye-patch, however, was about something more than nautical chic. 'I had conjunctivitis, so I made the most of it and dressed like a pirate,' shrugged Bowie. 'Just stopped short of the parrot!'

' David said, "I've got this riff and it's a bit Rolling Stonesy – I just want to piss Mick off a bit." I spent about three-quarters of an hour to an hour with him working on the guitar riff . . . We got it there and he said, "Oh, we'd better do a middle." So he wrote something, put that in. Then he sorted some lyrics. And that was us done. '

– Alan Parker, guitarist

LOVE AT FIRST LISTEN

I SAY IT'S HIP

> *Young Americans* is the definitive plastic-soul record. If you had played it to me five years ago . . . I would have laughed. Hysterically.
>
> – David Bowie

'Maybe you could believe Bowie was a gay Martian, a sensitive acoustic hippie, a futuristic zombie with a lightning bolt across his face. But a soul man? That's pushing it,' mused *Rolling Stone*'s Rob Sheffield. Then came the sultry, smoky cover art for *Young Americans* (1975). And Sheffield was undoubtedly forced to reassess his opinion. Clad in plaid, with not a trace of makeup to disguise his handsome features, Bowie looked undeniably, conventionally *good*. Once fiery and spiky as Planet Mars, Bowie's hair had lengthened and faded to carroty blond. Emerging from amidst swirls of smoke, he looks fresh from the Philly dance-floor – his only concession to his starry glam-rock past a glinting bangle at his wrist. Before long, hip-swinging hits like 'Fame' were filling discotheques around the known universe, and Bowie himself was being hailed as the most desirable Young American of them all.

> If you think the English can't dance, you want to see most Americans – or most white Americans.
>
> – David Bowie

> John Lennon ['Fame' co-writer] defined for me how one could twist and turn the fabric of pop . . . often producing something extremely beautiful, very powerful and imbued with strangeness. In 1975, we found ourselves backstage at the Grammys where I had to present "the thing" to Aretha Franklin. Before I'd been telling John that I didn't think America really got what I did, that I was misunderstood . . . So the big moment came and I ripped open the envelope and announced, "The winner is Aretha Franklin". With not so much as a glance in my direction, Aretha snatches the trophy and says, "Thank you, everybody. I'm so happy I could even kiss David Bowie." Which she didn't! So I slunk off . . . and John bounds over, gives me a theatrical kiss and says "See, Dave. America loves ya." We pretty much got on like a house on fire after that.
>
> – David Bowie

RUBBER SOUL MATES NEVER DIE

YOU'RE REALLY A FREAK. I DON'T MEAN THAT UNKINDLY

'Nothing you have seen or heard about David Bowie will prepare you for the impact of his first dramatic performance,' a voice booms ominously over the trailer for *The Man Who Fell to Earth*. Yet this sci-fi nightmare on celluloid – shot in 1976 and focusing upon hapless humanoid Thomas Jerome Newton – was not entirely unrelated to Bowie's earlier alien personas. Cooler

' David wasn't a person who ever expressed what he was feeling. He was very removed and quiet and this was perfect because my character, Mary-Lou, never knew what was going on inside Thomas Newton . . . Look at David: his skin is luminescent. He's gorgeous, angelic, heavenly – absolutely perfect as the man from another planet. I went to one of his concerts after we finished and thank God I didn't see him before the movie. I would have been in awe – a complete groupie! '
– Candy Clark

' I really came to believe that Bowie was a man from another galaxy. His actual social behaviour was extraordinary. He hardly mixed with anyone at all. He seemed to be alone, which is what Newton is in the film – isolated and alone. '
– Nicolas Roeg, director

than winter on Neptune and unreadable in the extreme, Bowie's Thomas is a figure of inexplicable magnetism, drawing love interest Mary-Lou to him with the gravitational pull of a small planet. For Bowie's big-screen debut, it was no easy gig. Yet, Bowie emerged as an uncannily appropriate fit. With his clipped tones and glazed-over gaze, Bowie playing the Thin White Duke playing an extraterrestrial stranded on Earth seems an entirely natural casting choice. 'My one snapshot memory of that film is not having to act,' confessed David himself. 'I wasn't of this Earth at that particular time.'

IS THERE LOVE ON MARS?

THROWING DARTS IN LOVERS' EYES

❛ I was frightened stiff by a lot of my characters . . . feeling them coming in on me and grinning at me saying, "We're gonna take you over completely!" The Duke was the most scary of the lot . . . He was an ogre for me. I hadn't seen England for a few years and when I got back there I found that I'd taken with me a character who was the epitome of everything that it looked like could be happening to England . . . I believe it was good – the best way to fight an evil force is to caricature it. ❜

– David Bowie

Clad in his uniform of crisp white shirt, midnight-black trousers and impossibly narrow waistcoat – cut to cling to the contours of his wraith-like frame – the Thin White Duke made his startlingly stylish debut somewhere between 1975 and '76. As described in 'Station to Station', the first glimpse of his pallid features and flawlessly slicked-back peroxide hair, was a truly 'magic moment'. Classically handsome and desperately romantic, Bowie's fans were instantly entranced – and then cruelly disillusioned. As with his tangerine-haired, hollow-cheeked twin Thomas Jerome Newton – a stranded alien merely masquerading as human – there's more to Bowie's haughty aristocrat than meets the eye. Crazed with power rather than love, the Duke embodies a particular kind of mania. Terrified of the chillingly creative force that he'd unleashed, Bowie fled L.A. for London and then Berlin. The Duke remained behind.

❛ I've come to interpret the drawing [Bowie's '76 self-portrait] as a tiny cry for help . . . a cry Bowie answered himself with the subsequent trip to Berlin and an entire lifestyle change. Bowie turned that dark period on its head, and went on to supply many more generations of fans with music and art and soul and inspiration. He careened beautifully into the future . . . where he will always be. ❜

– Cameron Crowe

DUEL PERSONALITY

' I always said it was a couple of lovers by the Berlin Wall that prompted the idea. Actually, it was Tony Visconti and his girlfriend. Tony was married at the time. And I could never say . . . and it was very touching because I could see that Tony was very much in love with this girl and it was that relationship which sort of motivated the song. '

– David Bowie

The second instalment in Bowie's Berlin trilogy, *Heroes* was recorded in 1977 in the elegant, echoing halls of Hansa Studios, a mere stone's throw from the Berlin Wall – a fracture-line dividing the city in two at its very heart. Like *Low* and *Lodger*, it is a perfect product of the city – as exemplified by the title track. A momentous melody that captures exactly the heady exhilaration of falling in love, 'Heroes' was inspired by all that Bowie witnessed of the secret world shared by two (apparently) nameless lovers. Every morning, he'd watch them meet by the wall. In the face of the couple's devotion to one another – and the rousing emotional momentum of Bowie's track – the manmade wall seemed altogether less permanent.

' I'll never forget . . . it was one of the most emotional performances I've ever done. I was in tears. They'd backed up the stage to the wall itself so that it was acting as our backdrop. We heard that a few of the East Berliners might actually get the chance to hear the thing, but we didn't realise in what numbers . . . there were thousands on the other side that had come close to the wall. So it was like a double-concert where the wall was the division. And we would hear them cheering and singing along from the other side . . . even now I get choked up. It was breaking my heart. I'd never done anything like that in my life and I guess I never will again. When we did "Heroes" it really felt anthemic, almost like a prayer. However well we do it these days, it's almost like walking through it compared to that night, because it meant so much more. '

– David Bowie

REBEL HEARTS OF BERLIN

YOU CAN'T SAY NO TO THE BEAUTY AND THE BEAST, LIEBLING

'He dressed in baggy trousers and dowdy shirts, and enjoyed the Berliners' disinterest in him. No one bothered him on the street, unlike in star-struck L.A. . . . Away from the limelight, he composed, painted and, for the first time in years, "felt a joy of life and a great feeling of release and healing", as he put it. He realised his goal was not simply to find a new way of making music, but rather to reinvent – or to come back to – himself. He no longer needed to adopt characters to sing his songs. He found the courage to throw away the props, costumes and stage sets. By the summer of 1977, Bowie was on a creative high. '

– Rory MacLean, assistant director, *Just a Gigolo*

By 1978, Bowie was ready to embark on his Isolar II tour, spanning 10 months, 4 continents and 77 monumentally memorable shows. In contrast with the emotive force of the music – Bowie's all-conquering anthem of love and liberation, 'Heroes', was a nightly fixture – the stage effects were pared right back to basics. Lit by stark neon lights alone, Bowie's costumes were shockingly, uncharacteristically understated. Gone were Ziggy's precarious, gravity-defying platforms and the Duke's super cinched-in suits . . . to be replaced with loose-fitting tees and voluminous, high-waisted trousers. A jauntily angled sailor hat was Bowie's one concession to his own kooky sartorial past. For once, he seemed more than happy to let his music do the talking.

'Life in L.A. had left me with an overwhelming sense of foreboding. I had approached the brink of drug-induced calamity one too many times, and it was essential to take some kind of positive action. For many years Berlin had appealed to me as a sort of sanctuary-like situation. It was one of the few cities where I could move around in virtual anonymity. I was going broke; it was cheap to live. For some reason, Berliners just didn't care. Well, not about an English rock singer, anyway. '
– David Bowie

ASHES TO ASHES, FUNK TO FUNKY

'What I like my music to do is awaken the ghosts inside of me,' Bowie reflected. And by 1980, the spectres of Bowie's former selves were being conjured by a new generation. Too young to remember them in the flesh, the Blitz Kids – a nocturnal breed who came to rule London's nightlife – were craving a little of the Duke's skeletal glamour or Ziggy's otherworldly

'When I originally wrote about Major Tom I was a very self-opinionated lad that thought I knew all about the great American dream. We had this blast of technological know-how shoving this guy up into space, but once he's there he's not quite sure why. That's where I left him. Now we've found out that the whole process that got him up there was born out of decay, and that it has decayed him . . . "Ashes to Ashes" is really is an ode to childhood, a popular nursery rhyme. It's about spacemen becoming junkies!'
– David Bowie

'I'm not convinced that I'm anybody's guru . . . I have a great imagination. I'm not a vegetable. I let my imagination run wild.'
– David Bowie

allure for themselves. With their deadly serious approach to dressing up, they were dazzlingly adept imitators. When tidings of their haunted visages and shocking neon crops reached Bowie himself, he couldn't resist spiriting four of them away (including scene supremo Steve Strange) to a beach near Hastings – his chosen set for the jaw-droppingly expensive 'Ashes to Ashes' video. Flanked by his Blitz Kid extras, Bowie marches ominously towards the camera, clad in a gaudy blue clown costume created for him by Natasha Korniloff, stage designer for *Pierrot in Turquoise*. An eerie conflation of past, present and future, the Blue Pierrot is easily one of the most sinister items ever to spring from Bowie's closet – and utterly appropriate for revisiting beleaguered astronaut, Major Tom.

PUT ON YOUR RED SHOES AND DANCE THE BLUES

'David's mime experience has served him well.
He can simply stand still for a section of a song, but
the shape and look casts a spell . . . many of those
moments are unique, not repeated even in a nine-
month tour. In Paris, a pair of red shoes were thrown
on stage during "Let's Dance". David danced with the
imaginary person wearing them, then took one shoe
and intently admired it in the palm of his hand.'

– Denis O'Regan, photographer

In Bowie's eyes, 'Life on Mars' – a surreally beautiful ode to mousy-haired muse Hermione Farthingale – is nothing but a starry, sci-fi version of Frank Sinatra's 'My Way'. And this is not all David borrowed from the legendary crooner. A decade on, Bowie's stage costumes – created for 1983's Serious Moonlight tour – seem lifted straight from the collective closet of the Hollywood Rat Pack. Impeccably styled in pastel tailoring, patterned braces, quirky matching Fedoras and dicky bows – undone when the mood took him – Bowie was every inch the gentleman. It comes as no surprise that Geeling Ng, the waitress who finds herself being romanced by Bowie in the video for 'China Girl', fell for her dashing co-star off-screen as well as on.

' He was unfailingly polite, charming and a gentleman . . . After the shoot, I got a call: "Do you want to come to Europe with me?" I knew it was a passing phase. I was 23, we lived in different worlds, but he gave me an experience that I'll never forget. We were whisked out of back doors of hotels, flying in private jets, David hiding from fans under a rug in the limousine. It was like being in the movies.'
– Geeling Ng

BIG LOVE IN LITTLE CHINA

I MOVE THE STARS FOR NO ONE

' Jareth is Goblin King. One feels that he's reluctantly inherited the position . . . as though he'd really like to be, I don't know, in Soho or something. '

– David Bowie

Bowie's decision to return to the silver screen in 1986 – in the guise of a capering Goblin King, one of the few human roles in Jim Henson's *Labyrinth* – provoked more than a few sniggers. But Bowie himself had the last laugh. Ever after, his cameo as Jareth (unfulfilled ruler of a multitude of Henson's gross-out goblin puppets) has served as a siren-song, drawing fresh fans in undreamed-of numbers. Jareth may be a child-snatching fantasist with questionable taste in trousers, but thanks to Bowie's preternatural charisma, he cuts an irresistible figure as he swaggers, struts and magic-dances his way through the twisting passages of the labyrinth. 'Do as I say and I will be your slave,' he begs of Sarah (Jennifer Connelly), the feisty teen come to rescue her baby brother from his clutches. The only real mystery is how Sarah can bear to refuse. For Jareth is no monster. In the hands of David Bowie, he's a mesmeric anti-hero – a leather-jacket-wearing Heathcliff dusted with more than a little of Ziggy's glam-rock mojo.

' I met David Bowie when I was fourteen and he became a hero to me – because he was an artist, and because he was a genius who had the time to be kind . . . the world will be a greyer place without him. '

– Jennifer Connelly

YEAH, I'M AFRAID OF AMERICANS . . .

By the mid-nineties, Bowie seemed finally ready to acknowledge his home planet. The cover of 1997's *Earthling* album features green fields, endless skies and David, presiding over the scene like a king – his shoulders draped with the most striking Union Jack frock coat. As with most items in Bowie's wardrobe, it's nothing less than a meteor-fragment of haute-couture history. Before Geri Halliwell rocked her own jaw-dropping flag dress at the 1997 BRIT Awards, David was pursuing a daring young designer by the name of Alexander McQueen. McQueen's response was typically nonchalant. 'David Bowie, innit?' he shrugged. 'He wants me to do tour costumes or something.' But he accepted the commission. And thus, Bowie's full-length flag coat was stitched into existence, complete with lacy black cuffs and strategically distressed patches. Utterly smitten, Bowie wore the custom-made creation everywhere from the stage (on tour with Nine Inch Nails) to the '96 VH1 Fashion Awards, signalling the beginning of a richly creative partnership between the two artistic renegades.

'There have been periods in my life when I have been so closeted in my own world that I would no longer relate to anybody . . . These days more than ever I feel like a very social animal . . . and I love the freedom of it; the joy it brings . . . the conflicts and the debates which go with being much more a fully active member of society. Sometimes I'm so happy I depress people!'

– David Bowie

DRESSED TO DISTRESS

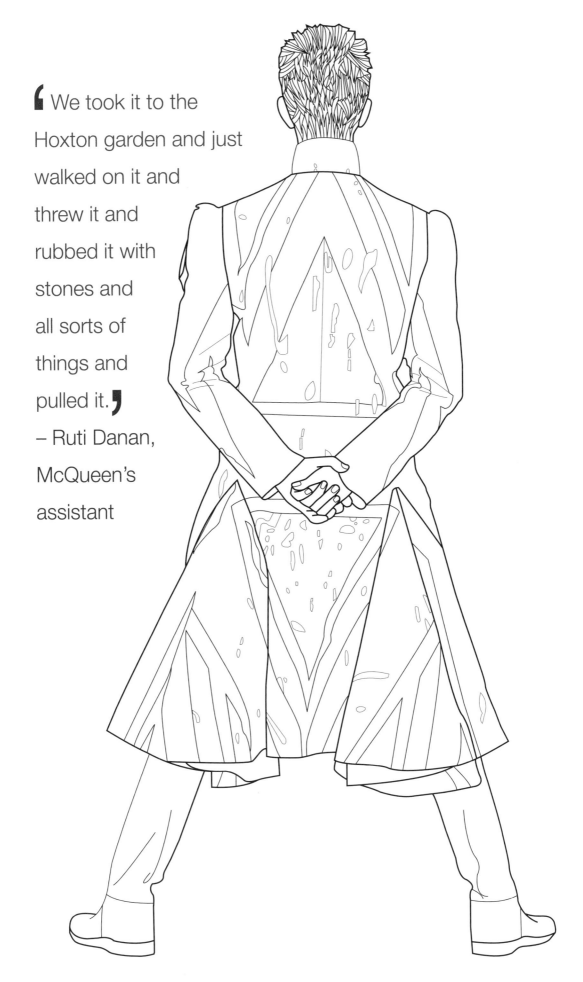

'We took it to the
Hoxton garden and just
walked on it and
threw it and
rubbed it with
stones and
all sorts of
things and
pulled it.'
– Ruti Danan,
McQueen's
assistant

GIMME YOUR HANDS 'CAUSE YOU'RE WONDERFUL

'Music has given me over forty years of extraordinary experiences. I can't say that life's pains or more tragic episodes have been diminished because of it, but it has allowed me so many moments of companionship when I have been lonely and a sublime means of communication when I have wanted to touch people. It has been both my doorway of perception and the house that I live in.'

– David Bowie

Bowie himself believed that, 'Ziggy is my gift to you'. But in truth no single persona could express his infinite contribution to the inhabitants of Planet Earth: past, present *and* future. Up

'He drew us away from our suburban lives, expanding our horizons, turning everything on its head, into gloriously subversive Technicolor. As an innovative writer, performer and rock star, there was no one and nothing else like him . . . A quintessential visionary, pushing the limits of his shape-shifting persona; the ultimate iconoclast, gracious, dangerous and legendary. The legacy of his extraordinary sound and vision will be loved and revered for as long as the earth still spins.'

– Annie Lennox

'He was the sweetest soul ever, with the best cheekbones . . . David, you were mortal, but your potential was superhuman, and your remarkable music is living on. We love you and we thank you.'

– Gary Oldman

until the very end, he never stopped creating; pouring all the energy he could muster into the compulsive process of writing, recording and producing *Blackstar*: his final, shatteringly beautiful accomplishment. Full of 'gentle throbs, ethereal rhythms and moments of stark introspection', it has been hailed by *Rolling Stone* as 'the greatest farewell in the history of rock'. In 2016, the BRIT Award for Icon was bestowed upon him by two of his close friends, Gary Oldman and Annie Lennox – both of whom spoke poignantly of his indelible, inspirational legacy.

BLACKSTAR ASCENDING

All rights reserved including the right of
reproduction in whole or in part in any form
First published in 2016 by Plexus Publishing Limited
This edition copyright © 2016
by Plexus Publishing Limited
Published by Plexus Publishing Limited
The Studio, Hillgate Place
18-20 Balham Hill
London SW12 9ER
www.plexusbooks.com

British Library Cataloguing in Publication Data
A catalogue record for this book is available
from the British Library

ISBN-13: 978-0-85965-550-7

Book and cover design by Coco Balderrama
Illustrations by Coco Balderrama
Text by Laura Coulman
Printed in Great Britain by Bell & Bain Ltd, Glasgow

This book is sold subject to the condition that it shall
not by way of trade or otherwise, be lent, re-sold, hired out
or otherwise circulated without the publisher's prior consent
in any form of binding or cover other than that in which it
is published and without a similar condition including this
condition being imposed on the subsequent purchaser.

Acknowledgements
David Bowie and his colleagues, family and friends have
given innumerable interviews throughout his career. These
have proved invaluable in writing and researching the book.
Thanks are due to: **Books:** Bowie, Angie, Backstage *Passes:
Life on the Wild Side with David Bowie* (1993); Carr, Roy and
Shaar Murray, Charles, *Bowie: An Illustrated Record* (1981);
Egan, Sean, *Bowie on Bowie* (2015); Leigh, Wendy, *Bowie: The
Biography* (2014); Pegg, Nicholas, *The Complete David Bowie*
(2011); Thomas, Dana, *Gods and Kings: The Rise and Fall of
Alexander McQueen and John Galliano* (2016); Thompson,
Dave, *David Bowie: Moonage Daydream* (1987). **Newspapers
and periodicals:** *Vanity Fair, Dazed, Uncut, Vogue, Variety,
Crawdaddy, Rolling Stone, NME,* the *New York Times,
Performing Songwriter, Disc* magazine, the *Telegraph, Elle, Stylist,
Entertainment Weekly,* the *Guardian,* the *Sun,* the *Independent,
Huffington Post, i-D, Melody Maker.* **Websites:** DavidBowie.
com, 5years.com, BowieGoldenYears.com, Feelnumb.
com, Bowiezone.com, openculture.com, Buzzfeed.com,
DangerousMinds.net, mashable.com, nme.com, motherboard.
vice.com, pleasekillme.com, troublemag.com, features.
japantimes.co.jp, elle.com, performingsongwriter.com, avclub.
com, ultimateclassicrock.com, theweek.co.uk, nydailynews.
com, recordsleeves.wordpress.com, pinterest.com, vam.
ac.uk, collections.vam.ac.uk, bowie-clan.tumblr.com,
hollywoodreporter.com, artblart.com, thesun.co.uk, sfae.com,
Reuters.co.uk, bowiewonderland.com, bbc.co.uk, moodboard.
typepad.com, timesofisrael.com, thosegirlss.blogspot.co.uk,
ibtimes.com, motherboard.vice.com, stylist.co.uk, i-d.vice.
com, dazeddigital.com, stolen-guitar.tumblr.com, YouTube.
com, dangerousminds.net, mtv.com, brits.co.uk. **Television
and radio:** *ChangesNowBowie* (BBC Radio 1, 8 January 1997);
Tonight, BBC, *Omnibus: Cracked Actor* (BBC 2, 26 January 1975);
Dick Cavett Show (ABC TV, 4 December 1974); 1975 Grammy
Awards (1 March 1975); *David Bowie: Hang on to Yourself* (BBC,
1996); *The Old Grey Whistle Test* (BBC, 8 February 1972); *Top
of the Pops* (BBC, 1972); *TopPop* (AVRO, 14 October 1974);
2016 BRIT Awards (ITV, 19 February 2014); 2016 BRIT
Awards (ITV, 14 February 2016). **Film:** *Pierrot in Turquoise/The
Looking Glass Murders* (Scottish Television Enterprises, 8 July
1970); *The Man Who Fell to Earth* (1976); *Just a Gigolo* (1978);
Labyrinth (1986); *Zoolander* (2001).

We would like to thank Sheryl Garratt for the
introduction which originally appeared in the *Guardian* on
11th January 2016.

We would like to thank the following photographers and
photographic sources for supplying the inspiration for the
illustrations: Cover: *Aladdin Sane* album cover. Brian Duffy/
the Duffy Archive/RCA Records; Dezo Hoffmann/REX
Shutterstock; Kenneth Pitt/Lindsay Kemp; Fab 208; Brian
Ward; Michael Putland/Getty Images; Masayoshi Sukita; Ilpo
Musto/REX Shutterstock; *Aladdin Sane* album cover. Brian
Duffy/the Duffy Archive/RCA Records; Masayoshi Sukita;
Pin Ups album cover. Justin de Villeneuve/RCA Records;
Richard Imrie/*Music Star* Magazine; *Diamond Dogs* album
cover. Guy Peellaert/RCA Records. The Estate of Guy
Peellaert; Peter Mazel/Sunshine/REX Shutterstock; *Young
Americans* album cover. Eric Stephen Jacobs/RCA Records;
Low album cover. Steve Schapiro/RCA Records; Gijsbert
Hanekroot/Getty Images; *Heroes* album cover. Masayoshi
Sukita/RCA Records; Barry Plummer; *Scary Monsters (And
Super Creeps)* album cover. Brian Duffy/the Duffy Archive/
RCA Records; *Labyrinth* film still, courtesy of the Jim
Henson Company/Lucasfilm/Henson Associates; *Earthling*
album cover. Frank W Ockenfels 3/BMG/RCA Records;
Jimmy King. It has not always been possible to trace
copyright sources and the publisher would be glad to hear
from any such unacknowledged copyright holders.

This book is not authorised or endorsed by David Bowie, his
estate or his record label.